NEW ORLEANS
CLASSICS

DRUMS

MUSIC MINUS ONE

5017

SUGGESTIONS FOR USING THIS MMO EDITION

WE HAVE TRIED to create a product that will provide you an easy way to learn and perform these compositions with a full ensemble in the comfort of your own home. Because it involves a fixed accompaniment performance, there is an inherent lack of flexibility in tempo. The following MMO features and techniques will reduce these inflexibilities and help you maximize the effectiveness of the MMO practice and performance system:

We have observed generally accepted tempi, and always in the originally intended key, but some may wish to perform at a different tempo, or to slow down or speed up the accompaniment for practice purposes; or to alter the piece to a more comfortable key. We have included slow-tempo versions of the most up-tempo pieces on this album for practice and/or a slower interpretation. But for even more flexibility, you can purchase from MMO specialized CD players & recorders which allow variable speed while maintaining proper pitch, and vice versa. This is an indispensable tool for the serious musician and you may wish to look into purchasing this useful piece of equipment for full enjoyment of all your MMO editions.

We want to provide you with the most useful practice and performance accompaniments possible. If you have any suggestions for improving the MMO system, please feel free to contact us. You can reach us by e-mail at info@musicminusone.com.

5017

CONTENTS

ISBN 1-59615-114-5

Drum Set

Fidgety Feet

Original Dixieland Jazz Band

Drums

Tin Roof Blues

New Orleans Rhythm Kings

MMO 5017

Royal Garden Blues

Clarence & Spencer Williams

Drums

Blue Orleans

Tim Laughlin

Dumaine Street Breakdown

Tim Laughlin

Drums

Savoy Blues

Edward "Kid" Ory

MMO 5017

March of the Uncle Bubbys

Tim Laughlin

Do You Know What It Means to Miss New Orleans?

Eddie DeLang
Louis Alter

Someday You'll Be Sorry

LOUIS ARMSTRONG

Quincy Street Stomp

Sidney Bechet

MUSIC MINUS ONE

50 Executive Boulevard
Elmsford, New York 10523-1325
1.800.669.7464 (U.S.)/914.592.1188 (International)

www.musicminusone.com
e-mail: mmogroup@musicminusone.com